THEOCRACY

TISH DAVIDSON

MC

MASON CREST
PHILADELPHIA

Mason Crest
370 Reed Road, Suite 302
Broomall, PA 19008
www.MasonCrest.com

Printed and bound in the United States of America

CPSIA Compliance Information: Batch #MEG2012-8. For further information, contact Mason Crest at 1-866-MCP-Book.

First printing
1 3 5 7 9 8 6 4 2

Library of Congress Cataloging-in-Publication Data

Davidson, Tish.
  Theocracy / Tish Davidson.
      p. cm. — (Major forms of world government)
  Includes bibliographical references and index.
  ISBN 978-1-4222-2143-3 (hc)
  ISBN 978-1-4222-9460-4 (ebook)
  1. Theocracy—Juvenile literature. I. Title.
  JC372.D38 2013
  321'.5—dc23
                              2012027863

Publisher's note: All quotations in this book are taken from original sources, and contain the spelling and grammatical inconsistencies of the original texts.

TITLES IN THIS SERIES

COMMUNISM	MILESTONES	MONARCHY
DEMOCRACY	IN THE EVOLUTION	OLIGARCHY
DICTATORSHIP	OF GOVERNMENT	THEOCRACY
FASCISM		

TABLE OF CONTENTS

INTRODUCTION by Dr. Timothy Colton, Harvard University

When human beings try to understand complex sets of things, they usually begin by sorting them into categories. They classify or group the phenomena that interest them into boxes that are basically very much alike. These boxes can then be compared and analyzed. The logic of classification applies to the study of inanimate objects (such as, for example, bodies of water or minerals), to living organisms (such as species of birds or bacteria), and also to man-made systems (such as religions or communications media).

This series of short books is about systems of government, which are specific and very important kinds of man-made systems. Systems of government are arrangements for human control and cooperation on particular territories. Governments dispense justice, make laws, raise taxes, fight wars, run school and health systems, and perform many other services that we often take for granted. Like, say, minerals, bacteria, and religions, systems of government come in a wide variety of forms or categories.

Just what are those categories? One of the earliest attempts to answer this question rigorously was made in the fourth century BCE by the brilliant Greek philosopher Aristotle. His study *Politics* has come down to us in incomplete form, as many of his writings were lost after he died. Nonetheless, it contains a simple and powerful scheme for classifying systems of government. Aristotle researched and illustrated his treatise by looking at the constitutions of 158 small city-states near the eastern shores of the Mediterranean Sea of his day, most of them inhabited by Greeks.

According to Aristotle's *Politics*, any system of government could be accurately classified and thus understood once two things were known. The first was, how many people were involved in making political decisions: one person, a small number, or a large number. The second issue was whether the system was designed to serve the common good of the citizens of the city-state. Taken together, these distinctions produced six categories of governmental system in all: monarchy (rule by one civic-minded person); tyranny (rule by one selfish person); aristocracy (rule by the few in the interests of all); oligarchy (rule by the few to suit themselves); constitutional government or "polity" (rule by the many in the common interest); and finally a form of mob rule (rule by the many with no concern for the greater good).

The fifth of these classic categories comes closest to modern representative democracy, as it is experienced in the United States, Western Europe, India, and many other places. One of the things Aristotle teaches us, however, is that there are many alternatives to this setup. In addition to the volume on democracy, this Mason Crest series will acquaint students with systems of government that correspond in rough terms to other categories invented by Aristotle more than two thousand years ago. These include monarchy; dictatorship (in Aristotle's terms, tyranny); oligarchy; communism (which we might think of as a particular kind of modern-day oligarchy); fascism (which combines some of the characteristics of tyranny and mob rule); and theocracy (which does not fit easily into Aristotle's scheme, although we might think of it as tyranny or oligarchy, but in the name of some divine being or creed).

Aristotle focused his research on the written constitutions of city-states. Today, political scientists, with better tools at their disposal, delve more into the actual practice of government in different countries. That practice frequently differs from the theory written into the constitution. Scholars study why it is that countries differ so much in terms of how and in whose interests governmental decisions are taken, across broad categories and within these categories, as well as in mixed systems that cross the boundaries between categories. It turns out that there are not one but many reasons for these differences, and there are significant disagreements about which reasons are most important. Some of the reasons are examined in this book series.

Experts on government also wonder a lot about trends over time. Why is it that some version of democracy has come to be the most common form of government in the contemporary world? Why has democratization come in distinct waves, with long periods of stagnation or even of reverse de-democratization separating them? The so-called third wave of democratization began in the 1970s and extended into the 1990s, and featured, among other changes, the collapse of communist systems in the Soviet Union and Eastern Europe and the disintegration of differently constituted nondemocratic systems in Southern Europe and Latin America. At the present time, the outlook for democracy is uncertain. In a number of Arab countries, authoritarian systems of government have recently been overthrown or challenged by revolts. And yet, it is far from clear that the result will be functioning democracies. Moreover, it is far from clear that the world will not encounter another wave of de-democratization. Nor can we rule out the rise of fundamentally new forms of government not foreseen by Aristotle; these might be encouraged by contemporary forms of technology and communication, such as the Internet, behavioral tracking devices, and social media.

For young readers to be equipped to consider complex questions like these, they need to begin with the basics about existing and historical systems of government. It is to meet their educational needs that this book series is aimed.

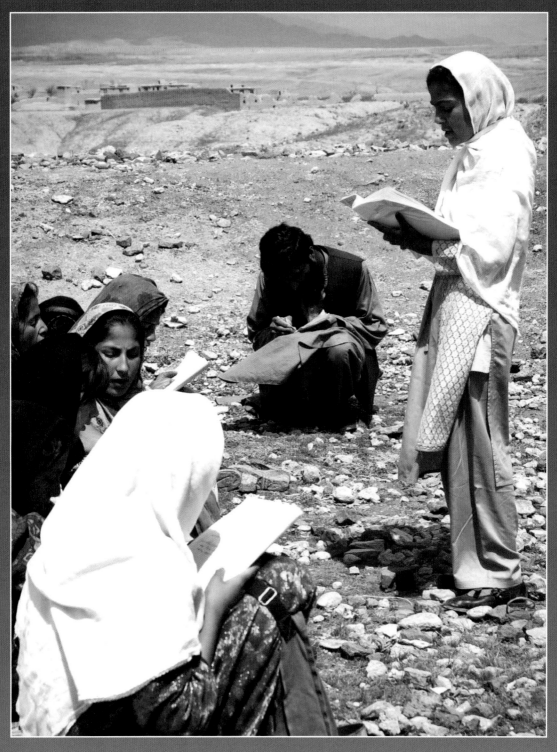

A young Afghan girl reads aloud to her class in a rural area near Kabul. The Islamist religious group known as the Taliban destroyed the school where these girls once studied and prohibited young women from getting an education.

1

RULE BY GOD

Kamila Yastali wasn't a police officer or a fire-fighter, but she nevertheless risked her life each day she worked. Behind the walls of her modest home in Kabul, the capital of Afghanistan, Yastali ran an illegal school. If the authorities uncovered her clandestine operation, she could be hanged.

Yastali's pupils also risked harsh punishment, for they too were breaking the law. To avoid attracting attention, they always arrived singly at their instructor's house, and they never congregated with one another or lingered on the streets of the middle-class neighborhood after the day's illicit lessons were done.

The stealth might seem appropriate for a spy ring. But Yastali wasn't training her students in the techniques of espionage, assassination, or sabotage. Her lessons were in math and science, literature and languages. What made the school illegal was that the students and their teacher

forth by the Greek philosopher Aristotle (384–322 BCE). Aristotle identified three forms of government (government by one person, government by a few people, and government by many people). Each of these forms had a pure and a corrupted variation, for a total of six possible government types. Thus, government by one person could be a monarchy (in which a virtuous king governs for the benefit of all of society) or a tyranny (an individual ruling for his own gain). Government by a few could be aristocracy (rule by the best, in the interest of all) or oligarchy (rule by the rich and well born, for their own gain). Government by many could be a polity, or constitutional republic (with citizens taking turns governing, for the benefit of all) or a democracy (in which all citizens voted directly, which Aristotle thought would lead to the masses of poor people acting for their own gain). In every case, the key factor was the person or persons exercising governing power, the actual rulers. In the theocracy Josephus described—a theocracy that would have existed perhaps 1,500 years before his time—the governing power lay with God, who wasn't physically present among the people. Moses led the Jewish people, but only as God's representative.

In the Bible account, Moses communicates directly with God. He relays God's instructions (as, for example, when he

Statue of Moses holding stone tablets that represent the Ten Commandments, the central principles of Judaism. The ancient Hebrew community is an example of a theocracy.

Muslims participate in Friday prayers at a mosque in Isfahan, Iran. Since 1979, a council of Islamic religious leaders has ruled Iran, making it one of the world's few theocracies today.

carries down from Mount Sinai the stone tablets on which God has inscribed the Ten Commandments).

In Islam, Muhammad ibn Abdullah plays a similar role as God's intermediary. Muhammad was a merchant in Mecca, a city on the Arabian Peninsula. Beginning in 610 CE, he reported a series of divine revelations. In those revelations, the angel Gabriel dictates God's words, which Muhammad is commanded to share with other people. The revelations form the Quran, Islam's holy scripture. Its content is quite varied. One important theme is the nature of God. Another is how people should live and worship properly.

In 622, Muhammad's followers—known as Muslims—were forced to leave Mecca. They settled about 200 miles to the north, in the oasis town of Yathrib. There, under Muhammad's leadership, the first Muslim state was established.

VARIATIONS

The stories of Muhammad and Moses illustrate one way theocracy has historically found expression: in the form of a government whose leader claims to have direct communication with God and claims to be relaying or revealing God's instructions to humanity. But theocracy is a diverse phenomenon. It has taken other forms as well.

For example, theocracies may arise in the absence of a living prophet. Islamic theocratic states were established in Iran and Afghanistan in the late 20th century, more than 1,300 years after the death of Muhammad. Jesus lived in the first century CE, but Christian reformers founded theocracies, among other places, in Switzerland during the 1550s and the Massachusetts Bay Colony during the 1630s. In cases such as these, scripture tends to be cited as justification for "rule by God."

COMMON DEFINITIONS OF THEOCRACY

Theocracy, which can take a variety of forms, is difficult to define in a comprehensive way. The following are only some of the accepted definitions of theocracy:

- a state ruled directly or indirectly by clergy (for example, priests, ministers, or mullahs)
- a state in which civil law is the same as religious law
- a government that requires citizens' social behavior to conform to religious law
- government by a leader who is believed to be a god or the human representative of God
- government by a person who claims to communicate directly with God and to relay God's instructions to the community.

Where polytheism (belief in multiple gods) exists, a different form of theocracy has sometimes arisen. Leaders have claimed to be, or have been regarded, as gods in their own right. Such leaders don't merely relay or interpret the divine will. As god-kings, they are part of the sacred realm. Thus, in theory their decisions as rulers are above reproach by their human subjects.

COMMON FEATURES

Variations aside, all theocracies have certain common characteristics. First, they occur only in societies in which a significant portion of the people believe in the existence of God or of multiple gods. For obvious reasons, a theocracy cannot be sustained among an atheistic population.

But theocracy also requires a specific kind of religious outlook—namely, the assumption that human affairs and human conduct are matters of interest to the Almighty. It's possible to believe in God while denying any divine presence or influence in the material world. The Deists of the 18th century, for example, said that God created the universe and its physical laws, then simply set everything in motion, never intervening in any way thereafter. These kinds of beliefs will never give rise to a theocracy. Theocratic regimes enforce conformity to rules regarded as divinely ordained. A God who stands completely apart from humanity is a God who doesn't reveal laws people must follow, and who neither rewards nor punishes humans for their behavior.

The idea of divine judgment is important in all theocracies. The way that judgment is understood, however, varies. Premodern cultures tend to view pleasing the gods as a collective responsibility, with consequences for all of society. If the gods are given their due, they will bestow rewards on society, or at the very least not interfere with its smooth functioning. But if people's behavior offends them, the gods will visit punishment on society. This typically takes the form of a natural disaster (for example, a failed harvest, disease epidemic, or earthquake) or a military defeat.

In modern societies, by contrast, it is more often assumed that any divine reward or punishment accrues to individuals, and for their own behavior. It is also commonly held that God punishes or rewards a person in the afterlife rather than during his or her earthly existence. Despite this, modern theocratic regimes don't give individuals free rein to make their own moral decisions. Instead, these regimes attempt to make everyone in the society follow the dictates of the dominant religion (as interpreted by the religious leaders who control the regime).

Modern theocratic governments have used various means to ensure religious conformity. Many have attempted to eliminate opposing viewpoints by controlling the educational system, by censoring the media, or by limiting citizens' contact with outsiders. Some theocratic regimes have expelled dissenters. That tactic was used by the Puritans of Massachusetts Bay Colony, and by the Latter-day Saints of Utah Territory during the second half of the 19th century. Other theocracies have resorted to far more coercive measures. The Taliban employed roaming "morality police" who beat, flogged, and sometimes even killed Afghanis found in violation of the regime's strict version of Sharia, or Islamic law. Offenders included men whose beards were too short; women seen in public not covered from head to toe in a burqa and accompanied by a male relative; and anyone dancing or playing music. Saudi Arabia's morality police, called *mutaween*, play a similar role in rooting out "un-Islamic" conduct in that nation.

AN OUTMODED FORM OF GOVERNMENT?

Theocracies have existed, at one time or another, all over the globe. And they have been spawned by a variety of creeds. Under certain conditions, almost any religion can give rise to a theocratic regime.

"THEOCRATIC, OR TO MAKE THE LORD GOD OUR GOVERNOUR IS THE BEST FORM OF GOVERNMENT IN A CHRISTIAN COMMON-WEALTH, AND WHICH MEN THAT ARE FREE TO CHUSE . . . OUGHT TO ESTABLISH."

—JOHN DAVENPORT, COFOUNDER OF NEW HAVEN COLONY (1639)

Nevertheless, theocracy has historically been a relatively rare form of government. And today it is viewed as outmoded in much, if not most, of the world. In Western societies especially, theocracy also tends to be seen in a wholly negative light. It is regarded as a repressive form of government, one that inevitably infringes on the basic right of individuals to hold whatever religious beliefs they choose.

Needless to say, not everybody living under a theocracy would agree. Government enforcement of piety may be seen as desirable in societies in which a large majority of the population follows the same religion, and the religion in question is understood to include absolute rules of human conduct.

Theocracy can thus promote social cohesion. There is little doubt it served that function in certain ancient cultures.

2

ANCIENT THEOCRACIES

In earlier times, natural phenomena such as floods, famine, the rising of the sun, and eclipses of the moon were attributed to supernatural beings or gods. Ancient peoples developed special rituals to please the gods and keep their communities safe. In some societies, people also believed that their king had special abilities to communicate with and influence the gods. When civil and religious authority was combined in the hands of one person, a strong theocratic government resulted.

Theocracy may have been fairly common among ancient societies. However, in all but a handful of cases, the archaeological record is very limited (or is nonexistent), so definitive conclusions can't be made.

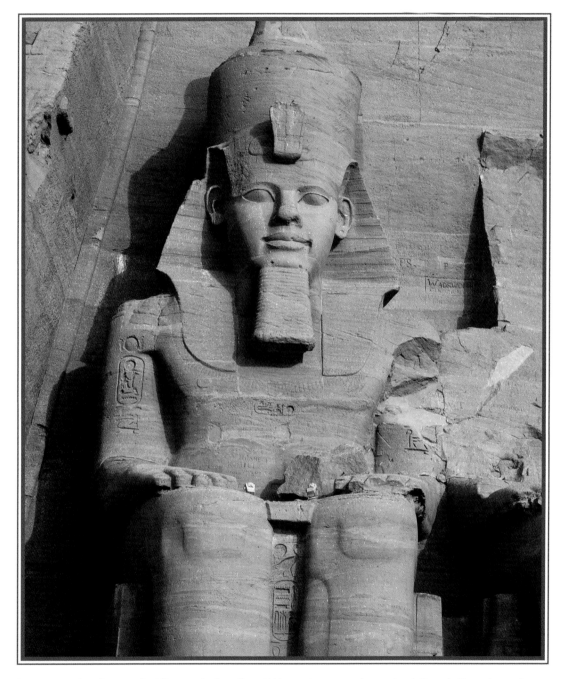

Ramesses the Great ruled Egypt during the 13th century BCE. In ancient Egypt, the pharaohs were believed to be divine, and their decrees could not be challenged.

Only a few ancient theocracies have been studied in depth. The ancient Egyptian civilization flourished for nearly three millennia in northeastern Africa. It left an abundance of written records and other artifacts from which scholars have been able to piece together the workings of the Egyptian theocracy, which was headed by the powerful pharaohs. In the Western Hemisphere, the Maya, Aztecs, and Inca also had powerful theocratic rulers. Knowledge of these theocracies comes not only from archaeology but also from accounts written after the Spanish conquests of the 16th century.

Many details about the Egyptian, Mayan, Aztec, and Incan theocracies may never be known. Still, scholars understand the broad outlines. As with all theocratic regimes, what gave the Egyptian, Mayan, Aztec, and Incan rulers legitimacy (justification to govern) was their supposed special relationship with the gods. But the Egyptian pharaohs, the Mayan kings, and the Aztec and Incan emperors were more than just representatives of the gods on earth. They were more than intermediaries between the divine and human realms. They were god-kings. When crowned, these rulers were thought to become divine.

THEOCRACY IN ANCIENT EGYPT

The Nile, the world's longest river, cuts through the vast and forbidding deserts of Egypt. The river's life-sustaining waters attracted human settlers from as early as 7000 BCE. Agriculture began in the Nile Valley some 2,000 years later. Farming was made possible by the river's regular flooding, which deposited (usually each year) a new layer of nutrient-rich soil on the surrounding land.

By the fourth millennium BCE, Lower Egypt (the Nile Delta region) and Upper Egypt (the area to the south) were controlled by two separate kingdoms. Around 3100 a ruler from Upper Egypt—probably Narmer—conquered Lower Egypt and united the two kingdoms. Narmer is generally credited with founding Egypt's first dynasty of pharaohs. Scholars believe that from his reign until 332 BCE, when Egypt was conquered by Alexander the Great of Macedon, there were a total of 31 dynasties.

Worship of the gods influenced all activities and all classes of people in ancient Egypt. The gods believed to control the sun, the moon, the earth, the sky, the Nile River, and all natural forces had to be kept happy. Two of the most important gods in the Egyptian pantheon were Horus and Osiris. Horus—usually depicted as a man with the head of a falcon—ruled over the sky, including the sun and the moon. Osiris, the green-skinned father of Horus, was god of the afterlife. He judged the souls of the dead. He also had another important function: to bring rebirth to the earth through the sprouting of plants in the spring. Osiris was a symbol of resurrection and eternal life.

In the Egyptian theocracy, Horus and Osiris both became associated with the pharaohs. When a pharaoh was crowned, the spirit of Horus was believed to enter him, making the pharaoh divine. The pharaoh served as an intermediary between his people and the gods, maintaining order and preventing chaos in Egypt. As a god he was considered infallible. When he settled disputes or made legal judgments, his decision could not be questioned. There was no standard written law. All justice depended on the decisions of the pharaoh.

During his lifetime, the pharaoh was worshiped at temples. He continued to be worshiped even after death. Pharaohs participated in all major religious festivals. Two of the most important were Heb-Sed and Opet. The Heb-Sed Festival was held after a pharaoh had reigned for 30 years, and it was celebrated every three years after that. The purpose of Heb-Sed was to restore the pharaoh's strength and ritually acknowledge his continuing right to rule. The Opet Festival was probably first held near the beginning of the 18th dynasty (ca. 1550 BCE). It celebrated the marriage of two gods, but also reinforced the idea of the pharaoh's divinity through a re-coronation ceremony.

Upon death, the pharaoh's spirit was believed to merge with the god Osiris and gain eternal life. In his eternal life in the underworld, the pharaoh would continue to protect the people of his kingdom. This made a proper burial very important and led to the building of the Great Pyramids and complex burial chambers carved out of cliffs along the Nile

River. Meanwhile, the dynasty continued with the crowning of a new pharaoh.

Not surprisingly, the religious beliefs of the ancient Egyptians evolved somewhat over the course of centuries. The importance of specific gods waxed or waned. New gods were sometimes added to the pantheon.

But one pharaoh made a radical break with traditional Egyptian religion. That pharaoh, Akhenaten, took the throne around 1353 BCE. Within a few years, he had replaced the worship of many gods with the worship of only one: Aten, the disk of the sun. After Akhenaten's death, his son Tutankhamun restored polytheism to Egypt.

Another aspect of ancient Egypt's theocracy deserves special mention. In about a half-dozen instances, women reigned as pharaohs. Female leaders—under any political system—were quite uncommon until modern times. In theocratic systems, women almost never rule, though there is also evidence for a few female rulers among the Maya.

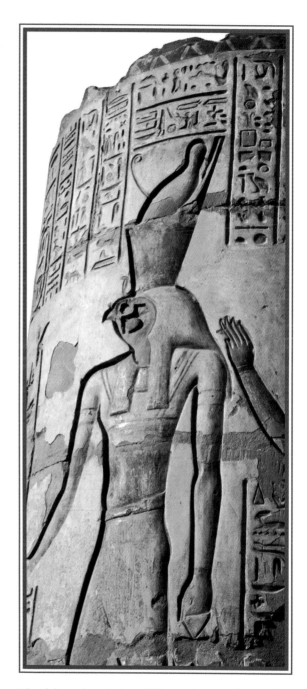

The falcon-headed god Horus is carved onto this column at the ancient temple at Luxor, Egypt.

MAYAN THEOCRACY

The Maya began farming in southern Mexico and northern Central America around 5000 BCE. By 2000 BCE, they were living in small city-states, each with its own hereditary king. Unlike the ancient Egyptians (or the Aztecs and the Inca), the Maya never developed a large, centralized empire. Instead, the city-state remained the primary political unit of Mayan civilization up to the time of the Spanish conquest.

The various Mayan city-states formed alliances. Some sought to extend their influence or attain regional dominance through diplomacy. The city-states also fought frequent wars. For much of Mayan history, however, these wars were limited in scope. Fighting was confined to soldiers, and

BALL GAME

The Maya and Aztecs, as well as other cultures in Mesoamerica, played a ball game that often had religious significance. The game took place on an I-shaped court that was usually bounded by sloping stone walls. The object was to hit a heavy rubber ball—without using hands or feet and without allowing the ball to come to a stop—over a center line to the opposing team's side. In some versions, knocking the ball through a high ring meant automatic victory.

The ball game was sometimes played just for recreation or entertainment. But it was also played as part of religious rituals. Among some Mayan groups, the game may have served as a reen-actment of episodes from a creation myth. For the Aztecs, the game may have symbolized the struggle between Huitzilopochtli (god of the sun) and the gods of the night.

The outcome of a ball game could have serious consequences for the players. Human sacrifices were sometimes conducted in conjunction with a game, and some scholars suggest that the victims might have included the captain of the losing team.

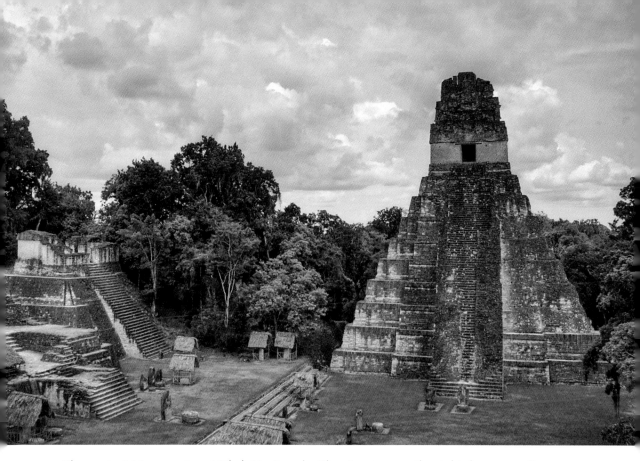

The ancient Mayan ruins at Tikal, Guatemala. The structure on the right, known as the Temple of the Great Jaguar, was the burial place of a Mayan ruler. It was built around 700 CE and is more than 150 feet high.

the main objective was to take enemy prisoners—including, if possible, the king. The prisoners would later be sacrificed to the gods. Conquerors typically demanded tribute, but they didn't destroy defeated city-states. Civilians were thus minimally affected by warfare.

Mayan culture reached its peak during the era archaeologists call the Classic Period, which lasted roughly from 250 CE to 900 CE. During the Classic Period, the Maya created stunning works of art and architecture, including massive stepped pyramids that were used in religious ceremonies and, sometimes, as tombs for kings. The Maya were accomplished astronomers. They correctly calculated the length of a year as 365.25 days. They also excelled in mathematics, using the concept of zero long before it was understood in Europe, for example.

The Maya worshiped many gods associated with nature, but beyond that their religious beliefs were complex. In the Mayan view, the universe was divided into three planes: the Heavens, the Earth, and the Underworld, also known as the Place of Awe. The Underworld, which could be reached through caves and subterranean rivers, was inhabited by a host of terrifying gods and demons. Mayan religious ceremonies—some of which included ritual human sacrifice—were supposed to keep those malignant beings from coming up to the earthly plane. Other ceremonies were performed to please the more benign gods, so that they would help the community. These gods included the Rain God, the Maize God, and the Sun God.

Like the pharaohs of Egypt, Mayan rulers were considered god-kings. They served as intermediaries between their human subjects and the gods. Mayan kings regularly offered their own blood to satisfy the gods. These bloodletting ceremonies involved excruciating pain. For example, one method of drawing blood was to pull a rope of thorns through the tongue.

Besides the god-kings who ruled the city-states, Mayan theocracy featured an important class of priests. They forecast—based largely on the interactions between the Maya's 260-day sacred calendar and the 365-day civil calendar—when the time was favorable for various endeavors. These included military campaigns, royal weddings, religious ceremonies, and the like.

Toward the end of the Classic Period, Mayan civilization began to crumble in many if not all places. Temples and monuments stopped being built. Important Mayan cities were abandoned completely. Scholars aren't certain what caused this cultural breakdown. Many theories have been offered. One is that agricultural production collapsed because of a long drought or unsustainable farming practices. Another blames a shift toward total warfare, with enemies targeting each other's civilian populations. Still another theory suggests that ordinary people lost faith in the legitimacy of their theocratic rulers, perhaps because of some catastrophe. A combination of factors may well have been at work.

Whatever the case, the Maya never again reached the same heights of cultural achievement. The Mayan civilization that the Spanish conquistadors encountered in the early 1500s was well past its prime.

AZTEC AND INCA

In contrast to the Maya, the Aztec and Incan civilizations were both at their height when the conquistadors arrived. The Aztecs dominated central Mexico. The Inca controlled much of western South America.

Both civilizations excelled in engineering and building. The Aztecs, for example, built their capital, Tenochtitlán, in the middle of a lake. The Inca constructed cities and an extensive road network high up in the rugged Andes Mountains.

The Aztecs and the Inca were both warlike peoples. Each carved out a large empire in a relatively short period of time. The first Inca ruler, Manco Capac, built a capital at Cuzco (in present-day Peru) in the early 13th century CE. It wasn't until about 1400, however, that the Inca began conquering neighboring peoples. In little more than a century, they had created an empire that was some 2,500 miles long and 500 miles wide.

The Aztecs, a small tribe of unknown origin, wandered into the Valley of Mexico during the late 12th or early 13th century. Tenochtitlán was founded in 1325, but construction of the city's causeways, canals, and monumental temples and pyramids required generations to complete. Until 1430, the Aztecs were dominated by another people, called the Tepanecs. Joining with two other city-states, the Aztecs overthrew Tepanec rule and founded an empire. Conquests during the next 90 years expanded the empire to the Atlantic and Pacific coasts. The empire was ruled by the Huey Tlatoani, or Great Speaker. He was worshiped as a god and had absolute power.

According to Aztec beliefs, Huitzilopochtli—the god of war and the sun—was engaged in a never-ending struggle with gods associated with the moon and stars. Huitzilopochtli required a vast supply of life-energy to sustain him in this struggle. Otherwise, the gods of the night would prevail. The sun wouldn't rise, and the world would be plunged into perpetual darkness. To provide Huitzilopochtli with life-energy, the Aztecs carried out human sacrifice on a massive scale. Victims—usually prisoners of war or people from conquered groups sent to Tenochtitlán as tribute—would be taken to the top of a pyramid. The victim's arms and legs would be held down as an Aztec priest cut open the chest, pulled out the still-beating heart, and offered it to Huitzilopochtli. (Human sacrifices were offered to other gods as well.)

Apart from the religious belief that they kept the world from collapsing into darkness, the Aztec sacrifices would have served a couple of political goals. The sacrifices certainly intimidated conquered peoples. They also reinforced the godlike authority of the Huey Tlatoani.

The Inca also practiced human sacrifice, but not nearly on the same scale as the Aztecs. Inca sacrificial victims were often children taken to a mountain peak, where they died of exposure. After death they were believed to become divine and to act as oracles, communicating messages from the gods.

Incan religion involved worship of many gods, as well as sacred places. Like the Aztec Huey Tlatoani, the Inca emperor—called the Sapa Inca ("Great Inca")—was considered a god. He was believed to be a direct descendant of Inti, the god of the sun. The Sapa Inca's person was so sacred that he was carried everywhere on a golden litter so that his feet wouldn't be profaned by touching the ground. All objects that the Sapa Inca touched were collected and ritually burned. This was to prevent ordinary people from touching anything that had come into contact with the god-king.

* * * * *

When a ruler is believed to be a god—like the Huey Tlatoani or the Sapa Inca—his subjects are likely to display extraordinary obedience and loyalty. This sort of theocratic government, history shows, can lead to highly cohesive societies. On the other hand, these societies can easily be paralyzed if their leader is incapacitated or the limits of his actual power are exposed. Peoples accustomed to following a ruler without question often founder when a need for independent decision making suddenly arises.

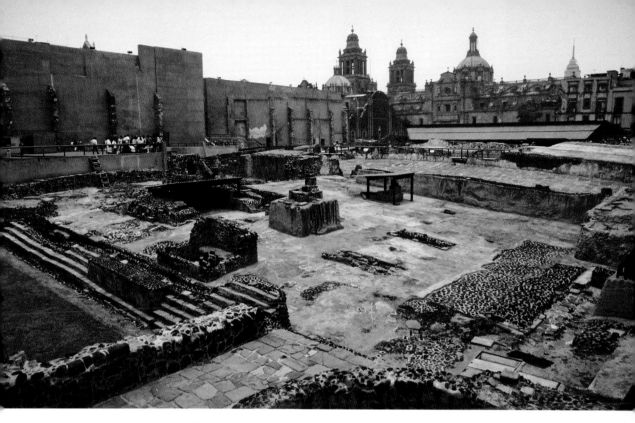

The ruins of the Aztecs' Templo Mayor (Great Temple), built in the late 1400s, can today be seen in Mexico City. The temple was an important religious site in the Aztec capital, Tenochtitlán. It included shrines to two major deities, Huitzilopochtli (the god of war and the sun) and Tlaloc (the god of rain).

This is well illustrated by the Spanish conquests of the Aztecs and Inca. In November 1519, the Spanish conquistador Hernán Cortés entered Tenochtitlán at the invitation of the Aztec ruler, Moctezuma II. Cortés had about 150 Spanish soldiers under his command, while the population of Moctezuma's capital is thought to have numbered several hundred thousand. But when Cortés made Moctezuma a captive in his own palace, Aztec society—including a mighty army that had vanquished numerous enemies—remained paralyzed for months.

The results were similar when the Spanish conquistador Francisco Pizarro met the Sapa Inca, Atahuallpa, at Cajamarca in November 1532. Pizarro's force numbered just 168, while an estimated 80,000 Inca warriors were encamped around Cajamarca. Yet Pizarro threw the Inca army into complete disarray after pulling Atahuallpa down from his gilded litter.

3

ISLAMIC THEOCRACIES

Muhammad ibn Abdullah, the Messenger of Allah, was both a prophet and a political leader. Born in 570 in Mecca, Muhammad said he received the first of his revelations from God in 610. At first, he shared the revelations only with a few family members and close friends. In 613, however, Muhammad began sharing God's message publicly. Gradually, a widening circle of people adopted the religion Muhammad preached: Islam.

Many Meccans were hostile toward Muhammad and the small but growing community of Muslims in their midst. Islam's central message is that there is only one God, to whom people must submit (the word *Islam*, in fact, means "submission"). Yet Arabs at the time were polytheistic, and merchants made a lot of money catering to the pilgrims who flocked to Mecca to worship the idols in a shrine called the Ka'aba. Muhammad also took Mecca's wealthy and powerful to task for their mistreatment of the poor.

Under the threat of violence, Muhammad and several hundred followers left Mecca in 622. They settled in Yathrib. There Muhammad demonstrated his skill as a political leader. He negotiated a pact with the Jewish tribes living in Yathrib. Among other terms, it committed the Jewish tribes and the Muslims to support each other in war. It also set Muhammad up as the final arbiter of all disputes. Yathrib was soon renamed Madinat al-Nabi, meaning "City of the Prophet," in Muhammad's honor. In English the city is usually rendered as Medina.

The Muslims raided Mecca's caravans, and intermittent fighting between the two sides went on for years. Meanwhile, the Muslim community came to dominate Medina as Islam gained converts, and Jewish tribes were expelled (or, in one case,

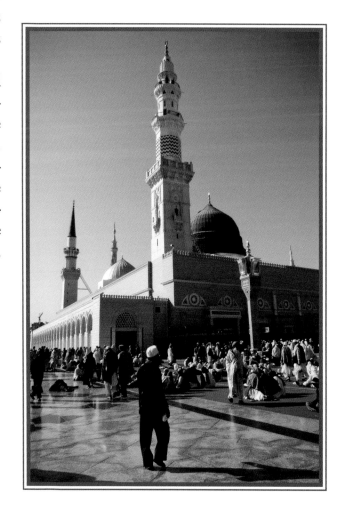

Muslim pilgrims gather outside al-Masjid al-Nabawi (the Mosque of the Prophet) in Medina, Saudi Arabia. The prophet Muhammad, who first preached the Islamic religion in the early seventh century, is buried under the green dome on the right. In Medina, Muhammad created the first state ruled by Islamic law.

slaughtered for supposedly conspiring to betray the Muslims during a siege by Meccan forces). Medina became a theocracy. Islam, as set forth by Muhammad, didn't simply serve as a guide for individual behavior. It also governed all social relations and was even the foundation of the state. "The Medinan community formed a total framework for state, society, and culture," observes John L. Esposito, a noted scholar of Islam. "It epitomized the Quranic mandate for Muslims as individuals and as a community (*umma*) 'to transform the world itself through action in the world.'"

In many ways, Muslims did transform the world. By 630 they had gained the upper hand on Mecca, and Muhammad and his followers marched unopposed into the city. Most people in Mecca converted voluntarily to Islam, and Muhammad established a theocracy there. When the Prophet died in 632, the entire Arabian Peninsula was under the control of Islam. In the century that followed, Islam spread—through conquest and voluntarily adoption—across North Africa and into Spain in the west, and as far as the Indian subcontinent in the east. Islam's realm covered more territory than the Roman Empire at its height. Many early Muslims viewed this as a validation of the essential truth of their religion. And because Islam is an all-encompassing way of life, many believed that their religion couldn't be considered successful in the absence of a flourishing Islamic state.

That attitude persists among a substantial number of Muslims today. In this respect, Islam differs from the world's two other great monotheistic faiths: Judaism and Christianity. For thousands of years, Jews lived as minority communities in countries all over the world. Often they shunned involvement in politics and government. In the case of Christianity, Jesus appears to approve the separation of secular and religious authority when he says, "Give to Caesar what is Caesar's, but give to God what is God's."

For many Muslims, however, removing religion from government isn't desirable. "In contrast to the belief in separation of church and state," write John L. Esposito and Dalia Mogahed in *Who Speaks for Islam*, "religion and society and faith and power are closely bound and intertwined in Islam. Throughout much of history, to be a Muslim was not simply to

The system of Islamic laws known as Sharia is based on the teachings in the Quran, the sacred scriptures of Islam. The Quran is a collection of the messages that Muslims believe Allah gave to Muhammad between 610 and 632 CE.

belong to a faith community or mosque but to live in an Islamic community/state, governed by Islamic law." It is for this reason, some Westerners have argued, that Islam lends itself readily to theocracy. But this view is at best an oversimplification. Of about 50 countries with majority-Muslim populations today, arguably only two qualify as theocracies. Still, when the Gallup World Poll recently surveyed 10 countries with predominantly Muslim populations, in four of those countries—Egypt, Pakistan, Jordan, and Bangladesh—more than half of respondents said that Sharia must be the only source of legislation.

Yet Sharia means different things in different places. Contrary to what many non-Muslims assume, Sharia isn't a set of precise, codified laws—as, for example, the United States Code. Rather, it is set of rules and principles derived primarily from the Quran and the *Sunna* (the recorded customs, habits, and practices of the prophet Muhammad). These sources date to seventh-century Arabia. Not surprisingly, they don't always address, in specific terms, issues confronting Muslims today. To take but one example, the Quran requires that Muslims (men as well as women) dress modestly. But what exactly does that mean? The Taliban interpreted it to mean that a woman in public must be covered from head to toe, with only her eyes showing. In Iran, by contrast, a woman must cover her hair but not her face.

THE SUNNI-SHIA RIFT

Variations in the way Sharia is interpreted lead to another important point. Islam—unlike, for example, Roman Catholicism—lacks an official head or worldwide hierarchy. In Islam no single figure has the authority to rule definitively on matters of faith.

During his lifetime, Muhammad was such a figure. As God's prophet, he spoke with total authority. According to the Quran, Muhammad was also the "Seal of the Prophets"—that is, the last prophet who would ever appear. Thus, it was understood that he could never be replaced.

Still, someone would have to lead the Muslim umma when Muhammad died. He failed to name a successor, and upon his death controversy arose. Some—who would be called the Sunnis—believed that the caliph, or temporal and spiritual head of the *umma*, should be chosen from among Muhammad's closest companions. Others—known as the Shia—thought that succession should be based on blood ties to the Prophet. They believed that Ali bin Abi Talib, Muhammad's cousin, should be caliph. Ultimately the Sunni view prevailed, and the first caliph was Abu Bakr, one of Muhammad's lifelong companions.

Though Ali became the fourth caliph, he—like the previous two Sunni caliphs, Umar and Uthman—was assassinated. The rift between Sunnis and Shia would become permanent after Ali's son Husayn tried to enforce his claim to the caliphate. In 680, at the Battle of Karbala, Husayn and his followers were massacred by forces of the Sunni Ummayad dynasty.

In the ensuing centuries, Shiism would develop some distinctive practices and beliefs. Today, Shia constitute only about 15 percent of all Muslims worldwide, though they form a majority in a few countries, including Iran and Iraq. Some conservative Sunnis regard the Shia as heretics.

SAUDI ARABIA

One country where Sunni-Shia relations are perennially tense is Saudi Arabia. Occupying most of the Arabian Peninsula, this oil-rich kingdom contains Islam's two holiest sites, the Ka'aba in Mecca and the Prophet's

Shiite Muslims march in observance of Ashura, a festival held on the 10th day of the Islamic month of Muharram. The solemn festival commemorates the martyrdom of Ali's son Husayn at the Battle of Karbala in 680 CE—a battle that marks the permanent division of Islam into Sunni and Shiite factions.

Mosque in Medina. While about 10 percent of Saudis are Shia Muslims, the other 90 percent adhere to a very conservative form of Sunni Islam. It is commonly known as Wahhabism, though many Saudis prefer the more generic term *Salafi*. Salafists seek to return Islam to its pure roots, which they define as the way the religion was practiced during the time of Muhammad and his companions and the two generations that followed.

The word *Wahhabism* comes from Muhammad ibn Abd al-Wahhab. He was an 18th-century Islamic religious reformer in Arabia. Abd al-Wahhab railed against what he believed to be the many ways Islam had been corrupted over the centuries. He rejected Shiism as well as Sufism (Islamic mysticism). Abd al-Wahhab allied himself with Muhammad ibn Saud, a tribal ruler from Najb, in the central part of the Arabian Peninsula. In the name of purifying Islam, they embarked on a military campaign. Between the mid-1700s and the early 1800s, much of the peninsula was brought under the control of the Saud dynasty. Eventually, the Islamic Ottoman Empire, based in present-day Turkey, was spurred to take action. An invading force from Egypt wrested control of the Arabian Peninsula from the Saud dynasty.

In the early 1900s, Abdul-Aziz ibn Saud, an ancestor of Muhammad ibn Saud, began reconquering the Arabian Peninsula. He completed that work in 1932, proclaiming the Kingdom of Saudi Arabia. King Abdul-Aziz didn't forget his family's centuries-long connection with Wahhabism. Not only did that form of Sunni Islam become the official state religion, but ancestors of Muhammad ibn Abd al-Wahhab filled the ranks of the *ulema*, the Islamic scholars who advised the king.

Today, more than 80 years after its founding, Saudi Arabia remains an absolute monarchy, with the king ruling by decree. For this reason, some people have suggested that Saudi Arabia isn't a true theocracy. But this begs the question. In Saudi Arabia, all citizens must be Muslims, and the practice of any religion other than Islam is prohibited. Civil law mirrors the ultraconservative Wahhabi interpretation of Sharia, which everyone is bound to follow. Religious police commonly known as *mutaween*—officially, the Committee for the Protection of Virtue and the Suppression of Vice—patrol public spaces and mete out punishment for Sharia offenses. These offenses include being in the company of a person of the opposite sex who isn't a close relative; the use of alcohol; immodest dress; and, for women, driving a car.

The *mutaween* drew international attention—and provoked outrage—in 2002. In March of that year, a girls' school in Mecca caught fire. But when the students tried to flee, they were blocked by members of the Committee for the Protection of Virtue and the Suppression of Vice. The reason? The schoolgirls weren't

In Saudi Arabia, women are required to wear a headscarf and veil, called a *niqab*, when they are in public.

wearing the long robes and headscarves required of women in public. At least 14 students died as a result.

IRAN

Like Saudi Arabia, Iran has large reserves of oil. That fact has played a major role in the modern history of the country.

Iran, called Persia until 1935, has a long and rich history. It has given birth to several major empires, beginning with the Achaemenid dynasty in the sixth century BCE, and it has been conquered and incorporated into other empires. For centuries, Zoroastrianism was Iran's dominant religion. In 636 CE, however, Arab conquerors overthrew the Persian Sassanid dynasty and brought Islam. Shia became the official form of Islam in the early 1500s, with the establishment of the Safavid dynasty. (Today about 9 in 10 Iranians are Shia Muslims.)

Iran's rulers wielded absolute authority until the 20th century. In 1906 widespread unrest forced the shah, or king, to accept the establishment of a parliament, called the Majlis. The shah also agreed to a constitution limiting his powers. In spite of these concessions, the shah did his best to thwart the Majlis. For years the legislature struggled with the king for power.

In 1908 a British group discovered oil in Iran and formed the Anglo-Persian Oil Company (APOC). The terms of APOC's agreement with Iran were highly favorable to the British company: Iran received royalties of just 16 percent on APOC's net profits. Many Iranians bristled at this arrangement, which they viewed as foreign exploitation.

In 1921 an Iranian army officer named Reza Khan staged a coup. Within five years, he had himself crowned shah, ruling as Reza Shah Pahlavi. He undertook a program to modernize Iran's economy.

Reza Shah declared Iran neutral during World War II. Concerned about the security of Iran's oilfields, British authorities asked the shah to expel all German citizens from his country. He refused, and in 1941 British and Soviet forces invaded Iran and deposed the shah. His son, Mohammad Reza Pahlavi, was installed on the throne.

In 1951 Mohammad Mossadeq, Iran's prime minister, convinced the Majlis to vote to nationalize the oil industry. British interests—particularly the Anglo-Iranian Oil Company, as APOC had been renamed—stood to lose out. Great Britain imposed a blockade, preventing Iran from exporting any oil. The toll on the Iranian economy was considerable.

The shah sided with the British in the oil dispute. By August 1953 widespread dissatisfaction with his rule forced the shah to flee the country. That exile wouldn't last long, however. With assistance from the British intelligence service, the U.S. Central Intelligence Agency organized a coup that removed Prime Minister Mossadeq and returned the shah to power.

In the years that followed, the shah tightened his grip on Iran. With American assistance, he set up a secret police organization known as the SAVAK. It spied on Iranian citizens and arrested, tortured, and in many cases executed people who expressed opposition to the shah's rule.

The brutality of the SAVAK was one reason many Iranians turned against the shah. But it was by no means the only reason. The shah and the rest of the royal family had a well-earned reputation for taking much of Iran's wealth for themselves. The shah's campaign to modernize and Westernize Iran—called the White Revolution—was also highly unpopular. Land-reform measures angered Iran's landowning elite while failing to improve the lives of peasants, many of whom migrated to cities. The traditional merchant class, known as *bazaari*, also felt threatened by the White Revolution's economic reforms. Conservative Muslims objected to political and social reforms aimed at improving the status of women. These included giving women the right to vote, compulsory education of girls as well as boys, and the adoption of Western fashions.

By the late 1970s, opposition to the shah's regime was broad based. But that opposition coalesced around a single Muslim cleric: Ruhollah Khomeini. An early critic of the White Revolution, Khomeini—an ayatollah, or high-ranking Shia scholar—had been jailed and then sent into exile in 1964. He continued to write and speak against the shah from Iraq and, later, France. He said that Iran must rid itself of corrupt foreigners and

Western influences and return to its Islamic roots. Inside Iran, Khomeini won support from Shia mullahs (educated religious leaders). His sermons, smuggled into Iran from abroad, were read in many of Iran's mosques during Friday prayers.

THE ISLAMIC REVOLUTION

Mass demonstrations, riots, and strikes broke out across Iran in 1978. The shah declared martial law and attempted to put down the unrest by force, but this backfired. The number of protesters only grew. In early January 1979, the shah appointed a liberal opposition leader, Shapour Bakhtiar, as prime minister. Yet this, too, failed to placate the regime's critics. On January 16, the shah left Iran.

Two weeks later, on February 1, Ayatollah Khomeini made a triumphant return to Iran. Millions of people crowded into the streets of Tehran, the capital, to greet him. Khomeini immediately made it clear that he had no intention of working with Bakhtiar, who had promised to bring democracy to Iran. Khomeini named his own interim prime minister, declaring that it was the religious duty of all Shia in the country to follow him.

Fighting soon erupted between followers of Khomeini and forces that remained loyal to Bakhtiar's government. On February 11, after military units began defecting to the side of the revolutionaries, Iran's top military leaders declared that the armed forces would remain neutral in the unfolding

The Ayatollah Ruhollah Khomeini (1902–1989) was an architect of the 1979 revolution in Iran that removed the American-supported ruler, Shah Mohammad Reza Pahlavi, from power. Once Khomeini and his followers gained control of Iran, they established a government in which Shiite religious leaders held both political and religious authority.

political conflict. That essentially marked the end of Bakhtiar's government.

The dizzying collapse of the old regime left a power vacuum. Local Islamic councils arose to fill the void, but in much of the country there was virtually no functioning civil authority. In this chaotic environment, a nationwide referendum was hastily held, on March 30 and 31. Iranians voted to approve an Islamic republic. On April 1, 1979, Ayatollah Khomeini officially proclaimed the founding of the Islamic Republic of Iran.

Many Iranians had yet to appreciate fully what that meant. Khomeini may have been the face of the Iranian revolution, the individual around whom the shah's opponents had rallied. But the anti-shah coalition as a whole didn't necessarily share his vision for a future Iranian government. In fact, few people knew precisely what his vision for a future government was. Most Iranians assumed that Khomeini would act merely as a spiritual guide for their country. However, he intended to create an Islamic theocracy—with himself at the head.

Former allies in the movement to topple the shah found themselves pushed aside by Khomeini's religious followers. There would be no broad-based coalition in the new Iranian government. Government posts were steadily filled with Muslim clerics loyal to the ayatollah. Those who objected were often subject to violence.

In late April 1979, Khomeini ordered an assembly to convene to draft a new constitution. His instructions were clear. "You are here to create a Constitution that is 100 percent Islamic," the ayatollah declared. "Not a single clause, not a single phrase can be devoid of the Islamic spirit."

The delegates did as they were told. The constitution they drafted, which went into effect at the end of 1979, guaranteed that the power of Iran's Shia clerics would be virtually unchallengeable, despite a veneer of democracy.

The constitution created the position of Supreme Leader—with Khomeini the first person to fill the role. The Supreme Leader is Iran's head of state as well as its top-ranking Islamic cleric. He serves for life. The Supreme Leader appoints (directly or indirectly) the members of a com-

The current flag of Iran, adopted after the 1979 revolution, reflects the country's status as a theocracy. The red symbol in the center is a version of the Islamic statement of belief: "There is no god but Allah," while the writing on the green and red bands, in the script used for the Quran, reads, "Allah is great."

mittee of Islamic legal authorities known as the Council of Guardians. Under Iran's constitution, this 12-member group has the authority to reject as un-Islamic any law passed by the Iranian parliament. Iranian citizens do vote for members of parliament and for president. However, the Iranian constitution requires all would-be candidates to receive the approval of the Council of Guardians. This gives the clerical establishment another powerful tool for preventing challenges to their authority. In 2009, for example, the Council of Guardians rejected nearly 500 presidential aspirants, permitting just four candidates on the ballot.

AN UNCOMPROMISING THEOCRACY

As Supreme Leader, Ayatollah Khomeini set about reshaping Iranian society. He systematically eliminated the Western cultural influences that had taken hold under the shah. Sharia was introduced, with much stricter limits on women's freedom. Morality police rooted out Sharia violations. Penalties were often harsh.

In the realm of foreign policy, Khomeini charted a confrontational course. He consistently referred to the United States as "the Great

Satan," and in November 1979, when militant Iranian students seized the U.S. Embassy in Tehran and took its staff hostage, his government refused to intervene. The American hostages were freed only after 444 days of captivity.

Khomeini actively sought to export the Islamic revolution abroad. In neighboring Iraq, he fomented opposition to the secular regime of dictator Saddam Hussein. In 1980 Saddam ordered an invasion of Iran, and a brutal but inconclusive eight-year war ensued.

Khomeini died in 1989. His successor, Ayatollah Ali Khamenei, has in some respects promoted an even stricter interpretation of Sharia. Under Khamenei, Iran's foreign policy has remained bellicose. Iran is widely believed to sponsor terrorist organizations, and President Mahmoud Ahmadinejad—first elected in 2005—has threatened to annihilate Israel. Iran's nuclear program, which most independent analysts say is directed toward the development of nuclear weapons, has triggered a variety of international sanctions. Iran's economy has struggled in recent years as a result of those sanctions.

Iran is a closed society. But there are indications of considerable dissatisfaction with the regime. For example, President Ahmadinejad's 2009 reelection—widely believed to have resulted from massive electoral fraud—sparked huge protests. In the end, the protests were put down violently by the government.

AFGHANISTAN: LAND OF PERPETUAL CONFLICT

Afghanistan, which borders Iran to the east, also produced a modern Islamic theocracy. But in most other respects, Afghanistan couldn't be more different from its Persian neighbor. Afghanistan lacks valuable mineral resources. It is very poor. It has almost no history of strong centralized government; loyalty to tribe remains of primary importance. About 80 percent of Afghanistan's people follow the Sunni branch of Islam.

Afghanistan has seen its share of invading armies throughout history. The extremely rugged terrain and fiercely independent tribal people have in almost every case brought grief upon would-be conquerors. For much of the 19th century, the British tried to conquer Afghanistan to prevent the expanding Russian Empire from cutting off Britain's India colony. In 1880, after two costly wars, the British abandoned the effort and settled for a treaty that allowed Great Britain to exercise control over Afghanistan's foreign policy.

In 1919, however, Emir Amanullah Khan repudiated that agreement and declared Afghanistan's independence from all British influence. But Amanullah's introduction of social reforms angered tribal leaders, who forced him to flee the country in 1929. Several years of bloody conflict followed before Mohammad Zahir Shah emerged as king in 1933. He ruled for four decades, until he was overthrown in a 1973 coup led by his cousin, General Mohammad Daoud Khan.

Daoud served as president until 1978, when he was assassinated. Communists seized power, but they were highly unpopular.

In December 1979, Soviet troops invaded Afghanistan. Their mission was supposed to be straightforward: to prop up Afghanistan's Communist government. But what ensued was a brutal, decade-long war. While Soviet forces controlled Afghanistan's cities, they weren't able to defeat Afghan guerrilla fighters known as *mujahideen* in the rugged countryside. The mujahideen—Muslim "holy warriors"—received weapons and money from various countries, including the United States and Saudi Arabia.

During the war, several million Afghanis fled the country. Many ended up in Pakistan. These refugees were never integrated into Pakistani society. To provide for the education of some of the refugee children, Saudi Arabia sponsored all-male religious schools known as madrassas. In these schools, Afghan boys were exposed to several strains of conservative Islam, including Wahhabism and Deobandi, an Islamic movement that originated in India and that calls for a rejection of Western influences.

THE RISE AND FALL OF THE TALIBAN

In 1989 Soviet troops finally pulled out of Afghanistan. Unfortunately, this didn't bring peace. The mujahideen continued fighting to topple Afghanistan's Communist government. They succeeded in 1992, but after that a bloody civil war broke out as mujahideen groups battled one another for control. Afghanistan was plunged into chaos. Former mujahideen leaders ruled parts of the country as warlords. They were corrupt and brutal.

In 1994, in Afghanistan's southern province of Kandahar, a small group of fighters seized and executed a warlord who had committed an especially heinous act. The group, led by a former mujahideen named Mullah Mohammed Omar, called itself the Taliban.

The Taliban appealed to many Afghanis by promising to bring order. The group's numbers swelled. After taking Kandahar Province in 1994, the Taliban set out to conquer all of Afghanistan. By September 1996, when the capital city of Kabul fell, most (though not all) of the country was under Taliban control.

Mullah Omar was declared *Amir ul-Momineen*, or Commander of the Faithful. The government was an absolute theocracy, with power concentrated in his hands. All government decisions would be "based on the advice of the Amir ul-Momineen," explained a Taliban spokesman.

> For us consultation is not necessary. We believe that this is in line with the Sharia. We abide by the Amir's view even if he alone takes this view. There will not be a head of state. . . . Mullah Omar will be the highest authority and the government will not be able to implement any decision to which he does not agree.

Under Mullah Omar, the Taliban imposed an ultra-strict version of Sharia. Women faced especially harsh restrictions. They were forbidden to hold jobs. They weren't permitted to go out in public unless accompanied by a male relative. When they did go out, women had to be covered from head to toe in a burqa and were prohibited from talking to unrelated males. Even laughing loudly was forbidden, as the Taliban believed that no stranger should ever hear a woman's voice. Because male doctors generally weren't allowed to see female patients, and because with few exceptions female doctors weren't allowed to practice medicine at all, thousands of women died in childbirth or from treatable illnesses.

Men had to grow beards longer than a fist. They had to wear loose-fitting robes and caps. Attendance at a mosque for daily prayers was mandatory.

No one was allowed to listen to music on records, tapes, or the radio. TV, movies, and the Internet were banned. Games and pastimes such as chess, dancing, and kite flying were outlawed.

Afghanis who violated the Taliban's Sharia rules faced harsh punishment. Women whose burqas didn't cover their ankles, for example, were whipped by the Taliban's morality police. Men whose beards weren't long enough were beaten. Women who were discovered wearing nail polish had their fingers cut off. Women accused of inappropriate contact with men were stoned to death.

The Taliban's policies outraged the international community. Only three countries—Saudi Arabia,

Mullah Mohammed Omar was the leader of the Taliban when it ruled Afghanistan, from 1996 to 2001.

Pakistan, and the United Arab Emirates—recognized the Taliban as Afghanistan's legitimate government. Ultimately, however, it was the Taliban's decision to provide sanctuary for Saudi-born terrorist leader Osama bin Laden that led to the regime's downfall.

Bin Laden—a financial supporter of the Taliban regime—had been living in Afghanistan for about five years when his al-Qaeda organization carried out the September 11, 2001, terrorist attacks against the United States. American officials demanded that the Taliban turn Bin Laden over to face punishment. The Taliban refused.

In October 2011, the United States and allied countries began a military campaign in Afghanistan. By year's end the Taliban had been routed—and Afghanistan's harsh theocracy was swept away.

4

WESTERN THEOCRACIES

In the Gospel of Matthew, Jesus draws a distinction between secular and religious authority when he says, "Give to Caesar what is Caesar's, but give to God what is God's."

Christians haven't always been content to keep religion and the state separate, however. In Europe, Protestant leader John Calvin created a strict theocracy in Geneva, Switzerland, during the 1550s. A century later in America, Puritans set up a theocracy in the Massachusetts colony. Mormon settlers did the same in Utah Territory during the late 1800s. All of these theocracies were relatively short lived. Theocracies headed by the popes of the Roman Catholic Church proved more enduring.

Thousands of pilgrims gather outside St. Peter's Basilica in Vatican City, the world's smallest independent state. The Roman Catholic pope is the Vatican's political and spiritual leader.

THE PAPAL STATES

By the early Middle Ages, the Roman Catholic Church controlled significant tracts of land, much of it on the Italian peninsula. But while the pope claimed spiritual authority as leader of the Church, he didn't rule a sovereign state. He wasn't head of a civil government. That changed in the eighth century.

In the early 750s, the Catholic Church was in conflict with the Lombards, a mostly pagan tribe from Germany that had ruled a large part of Italy for 200 years. In 753 Pope Steven II made an alliance with Pepin the Short, leader of the Franks, a tribe that lived in what is now France.

KEY IDEA

Theocratic governments enforce moral and religious values not only in civic affairs but also in their citizens' private lives.

The pope officially recognized Pepin as "King of the Franks." In return, Pepin sent an army to Italy to fight the Lombards.

After Pepin defeated the Lombards, he made a gift to the Church of some of the conquered lands. This was known as the Donation of 754. Pepin specified that the pope was to govern the donated territory as both a civil and a spiritual leader. These lands were the first Papal States.

Eventually the Papal States would stretch in a diagonal band across Italy, from near Venice all the way to Rome. For more than 1,000 years, the Papal States were a theocracy. They were ruled by successive popes of the Roman Catholic Church.

During the 1800s, the various smaller states that existed on the Italian peninsula were unified into the Kingdom of Italy. The process was completed in 1870, when Italian forces defeated the army of the Papal States and captured Rome. Pope Pius IX didn't officially acknowledge the loss of the Papal States, but the land was incorporated into the Kingdom of Italy. The pope continued to control a small parcel of territory atop Rome's Vatican Hill.

VATICAN CITY STATE

During the 1920s, the Church officially gave up any claim to the former Papal States. The Lateran Treaty, signed in 1929, compensated the Church for the loss of territory and established Vatican City as a sovereign state. This 100-acre realm, located within Rome, is an absolute theocracy led by the pope. Article 1 of the Fundamental Law of Vatican City State reads, "The Supreme Pontiff [the pope], Sovereign of Vatican City State, has the fullness of legislative, executive, and judicial powers." The pope answers only to God.

About 800 people live in Vatican City. Almost all are clergy or work for the Vatican. The Vatican has its own license plates, coins, postage stamps, and passports. When the pope travels to other countries, he is treated as a head of state, not a private citizen, and he has Permanent Observer status at the United Nations.

THE GENEVA THEOCRACY

In 1517 Martin Luther, a Catholic monk, wrote a list of objections to certain practices of the Catholic Church that he considered wrong. Luther didn't want to break away from the Church—he simply wanted to reform it. Nevertheless, the pope excommunicated him. But this didn't stop Luther from promoting his ideas, which spread across Europe and gave rise to a separate branch of Christianity known as Protestantism. The movement by which this occurred is called the Reformation.

John Calvin, born in France in 1509 and educated as a lawyer, broke with the Catholic Church in 1530. From then on, he devoted himself to the ideals of the Reformation. In 1535 Calvin moved to Geneva, Switzerland. There he established a church, enforced a strict code of behavior, and began to reorganize the city council.

Resistance to his ideas forced Calvin to leave Geneva for several years. When he returned, he formed a joint church-civil court called the Consistory. It disciplined people for violating church and moral rules. Twelve Elders chosen by the court became morality police responsible for monitoring citizens' behavior.

"It was as if the doors of the houses had suddenly been thrown open and as if the walls had been transformed into glass," one writer noted.

> From moment to moment, by day and by night, there might come a knocking at the entry, and a number of the "spiritual police" announce a "visitation" without the concerned citizen's being able to offer resistance. Once a month rich and poor, the powerful and the weak, had to submit to the questioning of these [morality police]. . . . For hours . . . hitherto trusted men must be examined like schoolboys as to whether they knew the prayers by heart, or as to why they had failed to attend one of Master Calvin's sermons. . . . They felt the women's

dresses to see whether their skirts were not too long or too short, whether these garments had superfluous frills or dangerous slits. The police . . . counted the rings on the victim's fingers, and looked to see how many pairs of shoes there were in the cupboard.

At first, there was some opposition to the morality police, but by 1555 John Calvin had almost uncontested power. He expanded the enforcement authority of the Consistory. Members of Calvin's Reformed church who were persecuted in other countries because of their beliefs began arriving in Geneva. This gave Calvin an expanded base of support. All who disagreed with him were punished.

After Calvin's death in 1564, religious control gradually loosened, and Geneva no longer functioned as a theocracy. Many foreign Reformed believers left the city and carried Calvin's ideas back to their home countries and, eventually, to America.

THE PURITAN THEOCRACY IN MASSACHUSETTS

The Puritans were an English Protestant group founded around 1560. They wanted to "purify" the Church of England, or Anglican Church. By the early 1600s, the Puritans—whose beliefs were almost identical to those of John

The religious reformer John Calvin (1509–1564) was the spiritual leader of the community in Geneva, a city in Europe that is now part of Switzerland. During the 16th century Geneva became an important center of Protestant Christianity.

Calvin and his followers—faced an increasingly hostile religious and political environment in England. In 1630 about 1,000 Puritans under the leadership of John Winthrop sailed to America. They followed a smaller group of Puritans who had crossed the Atlantic Ocean the previous year. The Puritans settled near present-day Boston and founded the Massachusetts Bay Colony.

Like Calvin, the Puritans believed civil government should follow the laws of God to ensure the spiritual welfare of the community. Also like Calvin, they believed in the doctrine of visible saints. Only visible saints—those people who could show by their behavior and testimony that God had chosen them to be saved—were allowed to be church members. The

CALVINIST BELIEFS

John Calvin preached the following beliefs in the Reformed church he established in Geneva. These ideas influenced many reformers who followed him.

- God is superior to all governments and rules the world with total and absolute authority.

- A literal interpretation of the Bible is all that is needed for organizing the church, the government, and private life.

- Anything not specifically mentioned in the Bible should be rejected; anything mentioned should be followed exactly without any room for interpretation.

- God chooses or preordains who will be saved at birth. Calvin called these people "living saints" or "visible saints." No one else can be saved, even by doing good works or living a pious life. People who behave immorally show that they are not visible saints.

Beginning in 1629 and 1630, thousands of men, women, and children made the two-month voyage from England to North America. They wanted to escape persecution and to manage their new community, the Massachusetts Bay Colony, according to their religious beliefs.

policy of excluding the "ungodly" was their way of strengthening religion in the community and making the government operate in the interest of their beliefs.

The Massachusetts Bay Colony was different from most other theocracies in that it had elected leaders (only free, male church members were allowed to vote) rather than a single tyrant who dictated and enforced the law. But like other theocracies it punished any deviation in belief or acceptable behavior.

The Puritan theocracy began to break down after the first generation of immigrants died. The infamous Salem witch trials of 1692–93 further eroded the power of the theocracy. Nevertheless, Puritan beliefs influenced the laws of Massachusetts for many years.

THE FOUNDING OF THE LATTER-DAY SAINTS

One other American theocracy arose from a new religion—the Church of Jesus Christ of Latter-day Saints, commonly called the LDS or Mormon Church. Between 1820 and 1827 a young man living in upstate New York, Joseph Smith, claimed to have had three visions. In the last, an angel named Moroni directed Smith to a hill near Palmyra, New York, and instructed him to dig up golden plates that had been buried there some 1,400 years earlier. The plates, Smith said, were engraved with a sort of hieroglyphic writing. Smith was able to decipher it with the help of special eyeglasses provided by the angel. Translated, the text on the golden plates became the

The Puritans excluded anyone from their community who did not wholly accept their beliefs. In 1635 Roger Williams, a Puritan minister, was tried in court for having dangerous ideas. His crime was to advocate the separation of church and state. Williams was found guilty and banished from Massachusetts. He went on to found Rhode Island, the first American colony to guarantee freedom of worship to followers of all religions.

Although Joseph Smith (1805–1844) established the Mormon religion in New York, he and his followers eventually left the state, settling first in northern Ohio and later in Missouri and Illinois.

Book of Mormon—sacred scripture as well as an account of the ancient inhabitants of America. It would form the basis of LDS beliefs and, in the view of Mormons, confirm Joseph Smith's status as a prophet.

By 1830 Smith had a small group of followers in New York. Encountering some hostility, they moved to Kirtland, Ohio, and later to Independence, Missouri. All the while, Smith claimed to receive many revelations from God. In Missouri, violent clashes erupted between the growing Mormon community and non-Mormons. Once again, Smith moved his followers, this time to Nauvoo, Illinois. There the Mormon community grew rapidly.

In Nauvoo, Smith reported a revelation that God wanted the Mormons to practice polygamy, or plural marriage. This proved especially controversial, helping to create a rift within the Mormon community.

In 1844 dissenting Mormons in Nauvoo founded a rival church. They published a newspaper in which Smith was assailed for his polygamy and accused of wanting to establish a large-scale theocracy, with himself as king. Smith responded by ordering armed followers to destroy the rival church's printing press. That provoked his arrest. He was charged with inciting a riot and, later, with treason against the state of Illinois. He was in jail in the town of Carthage, awaiting trial, when a mob killed him on June 27, 1844.

THE KINGDOM OF GOD IN UTAH TERRITORY

In 1846 Brigham Young, one of Smith's trusted advisers, led most of Nauvoo's Mormons west. Many would settle around Utah's Great Salt Lake.

The Mormon community at Nauvoo had been a theocracy, ruled by Joseph Smith and administered by a dozen of his apostles known as the Quorum of Twelve. In Utah, Brigham Young expanded theocratic rule. The Mormons, he said, were establishing the Kingdom of God on Earth, in preparation for the Second Coming of Jesus.

Joseph Smith had outlined the idea of "theodemocracy"—a blend of democratic practices with theocracy. Smith envisioned a government by God and righteous men.

Brigham Young claimed to pursue the goal of theodemocracy. On the surface at least, the Mormon community under his leadership did include democratic elections. However, votes weren't secret. No one Young didn't support was ever elected, and only laws he approved of were passed.

In 1849 Young petitioned the U.S. government to admit to the Union the Mormon "State of Deseret." This huge new state would cover much of the territory the United States had gained as a result of the Mexican War, including most of present-day Utah, Nevada, and

In 1854 the University of Deseret (now the University of Utah) introduced a new 38-character alphabet invented by George Watt, an English convert to Mormonism. The alphabet served two purposes. It culturally isolated the Mormon community, and it shut out non-Mormons. Despite repeated attempts by Mormon leaders to promote it, the new alphabet failed to gain acceptance.

Brigham Young (1801–1877) took over leadership of the Church of Jesus Christ of Latter-day Saints after Joseph Smith's death. Young led the Mormons west to Mexican territory that is now the state of Utah.

Arizona, along with parts of California, New Mexico, Colorado, Idaho, and Wyoming. The U.S. Congress balked, instead organizing the smaller Utah Territory in 1850. Young was appointed its governor.

Tensions between the federal government and the government of Utah Territory soon bubbled up. As non-Mormon settlers entered the territory, bloody clashes with Mormons erupted. Brigham Young was accused of failing to enforce federal law, and instead ruling Utah Territory as a personal theocracy. In 1857 President James Buchanan sent U.S. troops to Utah to impose federal authority. Brigham Young was replaced as governor the following year. After the outbreak of the Civil War in 1861, U.S. troops were withdrawn, and the Mormon theocracy once again gained practical, if not legal, control of the Utah Territory.

Brigham Young wanted Utah to become part of the United States, but only on his terms. In 1856 he wrote, "As the Lord lives, we are bound to become a sovereign state in the Union or an independent nation by ourselves." Utah Territory was repeatedly rejected for statehood because of its acceptance of polygamy and the absence of secret ballots in elections. Finally, in 1890 Wilford Woodruff, who had become LDS president after Young's death in 1877, issued a public statement rejecting polygamy. This and other concessions paved the way for Utah's admission into the Union. In 1896, when Utah became the 45th state, the vestiges of the Mormon theocracy that had once flourished were erased forever.

5

THE FUTURE OF THEOCRACY

The essence of theocracy is the imposition of one group's religious views on all members of society. Theocracies, by their very nature, limit the freedom of individuals. They punish failure to conform in matters of belief and in matters of personal moral behavior.

Theocracy is incompatible with the Western liberal tradition that grew out of the European Enlightenment, a wide-ranging philosophical movement of the 17th and 18th centuries. Enlightenment thinkers asserted the importance of personal liberty. They said that individuals should be able to live their lives as they saw fit (provided they didn't harm other people). Governments had no business telling their citizens what to believe. Everyone should be free to follow the religion of his or her choosing—or not to follow any religion at all.

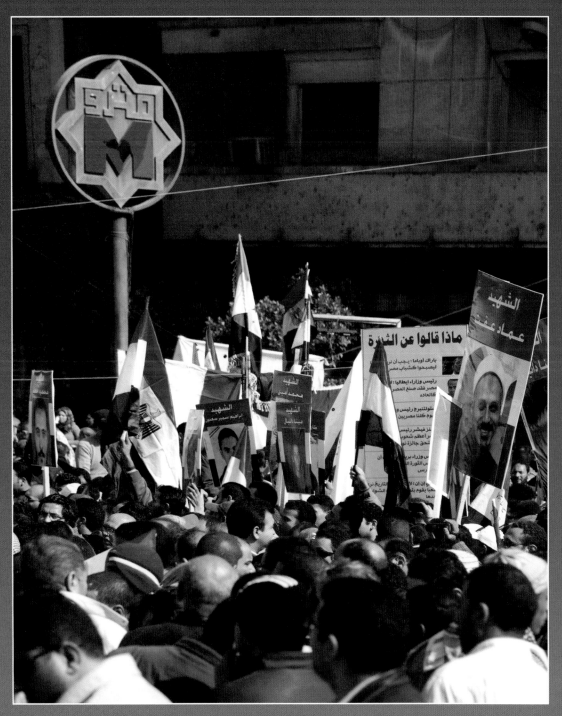

Some observers believe that the June 2012 election of Mohammed Morsi as president of Egypt could mark a major change for that country. Morsi was a member of the Muslim Brotherhood, an organization that wants to establish an Islamic theocracy in Egypt. Although Islam currently is the official religion in Egypt, in modern times the country's government has been secular, rather than religious.

Today freedom of religion is accepted as a foundation of all liberal societies. In many Western countries, it is explicitly written into law. In the United States, for example, the First Amendment to the Constitution guarantees that the government won't infringe on citizens' religious freedom.

OBSTACLES TO THEOCRACY

The United States—a nation of immigrants—has long been a very diverse society. Americans come from a multitude of ethnic and cultural backgrounds. They've inherited a variety of faith traditions from their forebears. Increasingly, other countries around the world are becoming similarly diverse.

Diversity of beliefs makes a theocracy much less likely to arise—or, if it already exists, much more difficult to sustain. Theocratic governments tend to be stable only when a large proportion of the people follow the dominant religion.

But even where an overwhelming majority of the population shares the same faith, theocracy won't necessarily be popular. In Iran, for instance, 98 percent of the people are Muslims. Yet in a recent survey by the Gallup World Poll, only 13 percent of Iranians said that Sharia should be the sole basis for legislation.

In the rare cases that a theocracy has arisen in recent times, it has always been in a country torn by war, political turmoil, or social upheaval. Chaotic conditions may make "rule by God" seem like an appealing option—as was the case in Afghanistan when the Taliban first emerged. Alternatively, such conditions may give potential theocrats space to maneuver their way into power—as, arguably, was the case in Iran during the Islamic Revolution.

In any event, circumstances similar to those that gave rise to theocracies in Iran and Afghanistan have occurred in other places. And on occasion they have led to attempts to establish theocratic regimes. Somalia, a country located at the Horn of Africa, is one example. In 1991 Somalia's central government collapsed. In 2006, after 15 years of fighting between rival militia armies, a group called the Islamic Courts Union (ICU)

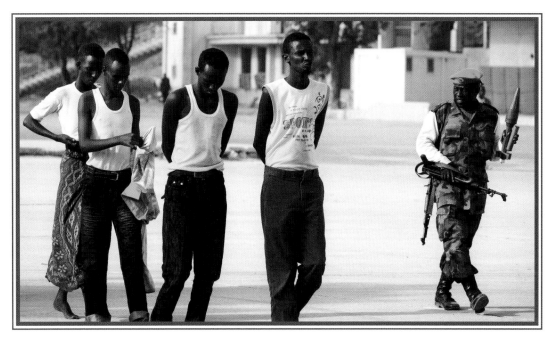

Four suspected members of the Islamist insurgent group Al-Shabaab are under arrest in Mogadishu. In recent years several attempts to establish a theocratic government in Somalia have failed to last.

established a theocracy in the southern part of Somalia. Although virtually everyone in Somalia is a Sunni Muslim, the ICU theocracy lasted less than a year. Beginning in 2009, another militant Islamic group, known as Al-Shabaab, imposed Sharia in the parts of Somalia it controlled. By 2012, though, Al-Shabaab had suffered a series of crushing defeats at the hands of African Union forces and troops loyal to Somalia's transitional government.

The failure of theocracy to take root in Somalia—where conditions would seem highly favorable to this form of government—hints at just how difficult establishing theocratic rule over a nation actually is. Still, the possibility that a theocratic regime may come to power in some other majority-Muslim country cannot be discounted. But it is highly unlikely that theocracy will spread very far. In the modern world, theocratic governance seems increasingly outdated.

CHAPTER NOTES

p. 8: "Some legislators have permitted . . ." Flavius Josephus, *The New Complete Works of Josephus*, translated by William Whiston (Grand Rapids, MI: Kregel Publications, 1999), 970.

p. 13: "Theocratic, or to make . . ." Avihu Zakai, *Exile and Kingdom: History and Apocalypse in the Puritan Migration to America* (Cambridge, UK: Cambridge University Press, 2002), 235.

p. 28: "The Medinan community . . ." John L. Esposito, *Islam: The Straight Path* (New York and Oxford, UK: Oxford University Press, 1988), 37.

p. 28: "Give to Caesar . . ." Gospel of Matthew 23:21.

p. 28: "In contrast to the belief . . ." John L. Esposito and Dalia Mogahed, *Who Speaks for Islam?* (New York: Gallup Press, 2007), 26–27.

p. 36: "You are here to create . . ." Saul S. Friedman, *A History of the Middle East* (Jefferson, NC: McFarland & Co., 2006), 292.

p. 40: "based on the advice . . ." Ahmed Rashid, *Taliban: Militant Islam, Oil and Fundamentalism in Central Asia*, 2nd ed. (New Haven, CT: Yale University Press, 2010), 102.

p. 44: "The Supreme Pontiff . . ." Vatican Information Service, "Vatican City State Has a New Constitution," February 1, 2001. http://visnews-en.blogspot.com/2001/02/vatican-city-state-has-new-constitution.html

p. 45: "It was as if . . ." Ronald Wintrobe and Fabio Padovano, "Spiritual Monopoly and Dictatorship." In Mario Ferrero and Ronald Wintrobe (eds.), *The Political Economy of Theocracy* (New York: Palgrave Macmillan, 2009), 101.

p. 52: "As the Lord lives . . ." Brigham Young, *Journal of Discourses*, Volumes 3–4 (1856), 40.

CHRONOLOGY

CA. 3100 BCE: Egypt is united under one ruler who is considered a god. This is the first known example of a theocracy.

CA. 2000 BCE: The Maya establish city-states, each ruled by a god-king.

CA. 250–900 CE: The Mayan civilization reaches its peak.

610: Muhammad ibn Abdullah, the Prophet of Islam, says he receives the first of many revelations from God.

632: Muhammad dies, having established Islam as the dominant religion on the Arabian Peninsula. Arab armies soon begin conquering under the banner of Islam.

1521: The Spanish conquistador Hernán Cortés defeats the Aztecs.

1532: The Spanish conquistador Francisco Pizarro seizes the Inca emperor Atahuallpa and routs his army.

1535: John Calvin moves to Geneva, Switzerland, where he later establishes a Protestant theocracy.

1629–30: Puritans arrive in Massachusetts, where they establish a theocracy.

1827: Joseph Smith claims to dig up golden plates on which are inscribed, in hieroglyphic writing, the Book of Mormon.

1844: Joseph Smith is killed by a mob in Carthage, Illinois.

1847: On July 21, Mormon settlers led by Brigham Young arrive in the Great Salt Lake valley.

1979: Mohammad Reza Pahlavi, the shah of Iran, is overthrown; under the leadership of Ayatollah Ruhollah Khomeini, an Islamic theocracy is set up in Iran.

1996: The Taliban capture Afghanistan's capital, Kabul, and proclaim Mullah Mohammad Omar Commander of the Faithful and leader of the government.

2001: On September 11, members of the al-Qaeda terrorist organization hijack commercial airplanes and crash them into the World Trade Center in New York and the Pentagon outside Washington, D.C. U.S. and allied forces attack Afghanistan and overthrow the Taliban regime in response.

2012: Al-Shabaab, an Islamist militant group in Somalia, suffers defeats at the hands of African Union forces and troops loyal to Somalia's provisional government.

GLOSSARY

BURQA—a loose, shapeless garment for women that covers the entire body and is worn in some conservative Muslim countries.

CALIPH—a successor to the prophet Muhammad as spiritual and temporal leader of the Muslim community.

CLERIC—a religious leader such as a priest, minister, pastor, imam, mullah, or rabbi.

COUP—the sudden overthrow of a government by a small group, often through violent means.

EXCOMMUNICATE—to officially exclude from participation in the sacraments of the church.

MULLAH—in Islam, an educated religious leader.

POLYGAMY—the practice of having more than one spouse at the same time; also called plural marriage.

POLYTHEISM—the worshiping of many gods.

QURAN—Islam's holy scriptures.

SECULAR—not religious.

SHARIA—Islamic law, based primarily on the Quran and the Sunna, the teachings and practices of the prophet Muhammad.

FURTHER READING

Berlatsky, Noah, ed. *The Taliban*. Detroit: Greenhaven Press, 2011.

Bringhurst, Newell. *Brigham Young and the Expanding American Frontier.* Boston: Little, Brown, 1986.

Goldstein, Natalie. *Religion and the State*. New York: Facts on File, 2010.

Latifa, with Shekeba Hachemi. *My Forbidden Face: Growing up Under the Taliban: A Young Woman's Story.* New York: Hyperion, 2001.

Morgan, Edmund S. *The Puritan Dilemma: The Story of John Winthrop.* 3rd ed. New York: Pearson Longman, 2007.

Perl, Lila. *Theocracy*. Tarrytown, NY: Marshall Cavendish, 2008.

INTERNET RESOURCES

http://www.newadvent.org/cathen

> This Internet version of the Catholic Encyclopedia—published originally in 1913—provides articles on a variety of subjects related to the Roman Catholic Church.

http://www.pbs.org/empires/islam/

> The companion website for the PBS documentary film *Islam: Empire of Faith* contains a wealth of information about the history of Islam.

http://www.pbs.org/mormons/

> An introduction to the Church of Jesus Christ of Latter-day Saints, from the PBS series *American Experience*.

INDEX

Abd al-Wahhab, Muhammad ibn, 31, 32
Abdul-Aziz ibn Saud. *See* Ibn Saud (King Abdul-Aziz ibn Saud)
Abu Bakr (caliph), 30
Afghanistan, *6*, 7–8, 11, 13, 38–41, 56
Ahmadinejad, Mahmoud, 38
Akhenaten (Pharaoh), 19
al-Qaeda, 41
Al-Shabaab, 57
Alexander the Great, 17
Ali bin Abi Talib (caliph), 30, *31*
Aristotle, 9
Atahuallpa (Sapa Inca), 25
Aztecs, 17, 20, 23–25

Bakhtiar, Shapour, 35–36
Bin Laden, Osama, 41
Buchanan, James, 52

Calvin, John, 42, 45–47
Christianity, 11, 28, 42
  and the Papal States, 43–44
  and Protestantism, 45–47, *48*, 49
Church of Jesus Christ of Latter-day Saints. *See* Mormon Church
Classic Period (Maya), 21, 22
Cortés, Hernán, 25

Davenport, John, 13

Egypt, *16*, 17–19, 29, 31, *55*
Esposito, John L., 28–29

Geneva theocracy (Switzerland), 11, 42, 45–46, 47

Horus (Egyptian god), 18, 19
Huey Tlatoani, 23, 24
Huitzilopochtli (Aztec god), 20, 23–24, *25*
human sacrifice, 20, 21, 22, 24
Husayn, 30, *31*
Hussein, Saddam, 38

Ibn Saud (King Abdul-Aziz ibn Saud), 31–32
ibn Saud, Muhammad, 31
Inca, 17, 23, 24–25
Iran, 11, 30, 33–35, 37–38

and the Islamic Revolution, 35–36, 56
  and Sharia, 29, 56
Iraq, 30, 38
Islam, 10, 26–29, *55*
  in Afghanistan, *6*, 7–8, 11, 13, 38–41, 56
  in Iran, 11, 29, 30, 33–38, 56
  and Sharia, 29, 30, 32, 37, 40, 41, 56, 57
  Shia-Sunni rift in, 30–31, 33, 38
  in Somalia, 56–57
  and Wahhabism, 31–32, 39
Islamic Revolution, 35–36, 56
  See also Iran

Jesus, 11, 28, 42
  See also Christianity
Josephus, 8, 9
Judaism, 8–9, 27, 28

Khamenei, Ali (Ayatollah), 38
Khan, Amanullah (Emir), 39
Khan, Mohammad Daoud, 39
Khomeini, Ruhollah (Ayatollah), 34–36, 37–38

Latter-day Saints. *See* Mormon Church
Lombards (tribe), 43–44
Luther, Martin, 45

Madinat al-Nabi. *See* Medina
Maize God (Maya), 22
Manco Capac, 23
Massachusetts Bay Colony, 11, 13, 42, 46–47, *48*, 49
Maya, 17, 20–23
Mecca, 10, 26–27, 28, 30
Medina, 27–28, 31
Moctezuma II, 25
Mogahed, Dalia, 28–29
Mohammad Reza Pahlavi, 33, 34, 35
Mormon Church, 13, 42, 49–53
Morsi, Mohammed, *55*
Moses, 8, 9–10, 11
Mossadeq, Mohammad, 34
Muhammad, 10–11, 26–28, 29, 30
  See also Islam
mujahideen, 39–40
  See also Afghanistan

Muslim Brotherhood, *55*
Muslims. *See* Islam
mutaween, 13, 32–33
  See also Saudi Arabia

Narmer (Pharaoh), 17

Omar, Mohammed (Mullah), 40, *41*
Osiris (Egyptian god), 18

Pahlavi, Mohammad Reza. *See* Mohammad Reza Pahlavi
Pahlavi, Reza Shah. *See* Reza Shah Pahlavi
Papal States, 43–44
  See also Christianity
Pepin the Short, 43–44
pharaohs, 17–19
  See also Egypt
Pizarro, Francisco, 25
polytheism, 12, 26
Puritans, 13, 42, 46–47, *48*, 49
  See also Christianity

Quran, 10, 29, 30
  See also Islam

Rain God (Maya), 22
Ramesses the Great, *16*
Reza Shah Pahlavi, 33

Salafi. *See* Wahhabism
Sapa Inca, 24, 25
Saudi Arabia, 13, 30–33, 41
Shah, Mohammad Zahir, 39
Sharia, 29, 30, 32, 37, 40, 41, 56, 57
  See also Islam
Smith, Joseph, 49–51, *52*
  See also Mormon Church
Somalia, 56–57
Steven II (Pope), 43–44
Sun God (Maya), 22
Switzerland, 11, 42, 45–46, 47

Taliban, *6*, 7–8, 13, 29, 39–41, 56
  See also Afghanistan
Tenochtitlán, 23, 24, 25
Tepanecs, 23
terrorism, 41, *57*
theocracy, 8–12, 13–15

Numbers in **bold italics** refer to captions.

in Afghanistan, *6*, 7–8, 11, 13,
38–41, 56
in Africa, 56–57
in America, 11, 13, 42, 46–47,
48, 49–53, 56
in ancient civilizations, 15–25
characteristics of, 12–13
definition of, 8–9, 11
in Europe, 11, 42, 43–46, 47
future of, 54, 56
in Iran, 11, 29, 30, 33–38, 56
and women rulers, 19
Tlaloc (Aztec god), *25*
Tutankhamum (Pharaoh), 19

Umar (caliph), 30
University of Deseret (University of
Utah), 51
Uthman (caliph), 30

Vatican City, *43*, 44–45

Wahhabism, 31–32, 39
See also Islam
Watt, George, 51
Williams, Roger, 49
Winthrop, John, 47
Woodruff, Wilford, 53

Yastali, Kamila, 7
Yathrib. *See* Medina
Young, Brigham, 51–53
See also Mormon Church

CONTRIBUTORS

Senior Consulting Editor TIMOTHY J. COLTON is Morris and Anna Feldberg Professor of Government and Russian Studies and is the chair of the Department of Government at Harvard University. His books include *The Dilemma of Reform in the Soviet Union* (1986); *Moscow: Governing the Socialist Metropolis* (1995), which was named best scholarly book in government and political science by the Association of American Publishers; *Transitional Citizens: Voters and What Influences Them in the New Russia* (2000); and *Popular Choice and Managed Democracy: The Russian Elections of 1999 and 2000* (with Michael McFaul, 2003). Dr. Colton is a member of the editorial board of World Politics and Post-Soviet Affairs.

TISH DAVIDSON has written many articles for newspapers and magazines. Her books for middle school readers include *School Conflict, Prejudice,* and *Facing Competition.* She was chosen a *California Readers* author of the month for September 2010. Davidson lives in Fremont, California, and is a volunteer puppy raiser for Guide Dogs for the Blind.

PICTURE CREDITS: © 2012 Photos.com, a division of Getty Images: 25, 37, 46, 48; Library of Congress: 50, 52; used under license from Shutterstock, Inc.: 1, 9, 10, 16, 19, 21, 29, 32; Mohamed Elsayyed / Shutterstock.com: 55; Georgios Kollidas / Shutterstock.com: 35; Jan Kranendonk / Shutterstock.com: 31; Tupungato / Shutterstock.com: 43; Ahmad Faizal Yahya / Shutterstock.com: 27; U.N. Photo: 57; U.S. Department of Defense: 6; U.S. Department of Homeland Security: 41.